LOOKING BACK,

THEN MOVING FOWARD!

CELESTE CUFFIE

2nd Edition

Looking Back, Then Moving Forward!

Celeste Cuffie

2nd Edition

www.celestecuffie.com

Twitter-@Celesteempowers

ISBN-13: 978-1535548250

ISBN-10: 1535548258

Cover Image- Jo Ann Snover. 123.rf.com.

Author Photograph- Clinton Campbell

In Memory Of

Tom Stevens

Jonathan Cuffie

Tina Cowan Wynn

Rose Stevens

Florida Sheppard

"I have to treat fear like tears. I have to accept it, embrace it and then do what I need to do. If tears don't stop women from giving birth, if tears didn't stop my mom from burying my dad, then fear shouldn't stop me from moving forward in my life. Fear is now my motivation."

Celeste Cuffie

Chapter One

That Which Doesn't Kill You...

Finally, I am beginning this new chapter in my life. I've wanted to write for years. Something that would share what's inside of me with the world. Something that would help encourage, support, and /or motivate others to move closer to their dreams, goals, hopes, and aspirations, in despite of their obstacles.

Isn't fear a funny thing? It is funny yet captivating. The fear of accomplishing something that you have never accomplished can be so overwhelming that you don't even attempt to try. However, when you try, you at least will finish with a success or fail. But if you don't simply try, it's a simple fail.

So here I am simply trying. Regardless of my fears, my inexperience, and my lack of confidence in this area ... I am trying. Nothing beats a failure but a try.

Reflecting on my career and the highs and lows of it, I am trying to make sense of it all. What have I learned from being a newspaper delivery girl, a waitress, a nursing assistant, a bank lady, and a business analyst? What can I take away, now that I have been laid off from the two positions in Corporate America that I loved most? Where does my value lie and where can it be deposited into, now that I have an associate's degree, a bachelor's degree, and a master's degree? What now? What lessons do I get from these experiences?

I am sure if you have been through a job loss, the loss of a loved one, a near death experience, or something that the insurance industry would call "a major life change," you have asked yourself these same questions. What now? What's next? What did I learn from it? What was I supposed to learn from it? And more important, who can I teach and empower as a result of it? That which doesn't kill you will make you stronger—a very true statement that I have heard, believe and have shared often, but more importantly, it can also make others stronger.

It doesn't matter how you are taught through books, people, and other resources to handle situations, you can't really embrace the knowledge until you are actually faced with them. It is best to have the teaching embedded within you, so when you encounter situations, you can at least draw from your knowledge base.

Chapter Two

Tears are a Sign of Strength

In this last experience in being terminated from my job, I remember being in a meeting and getting a call from my manager's manager. He, "Sam," took over this position about six months before this sunny, spring day occurred; yet, this was the only time I sat in an office with him besides on the day he introduced himself to the team.

With the changes going on in the organization, I should have known that it was coming; but I believed that my role was critical to the organization. Either way, I ended up in the office with him. What's also interesting is that while I was in an earlier scheduled meeting, my manager himself was also being let go. He often assured me that my role, our roles, were critical. Guess not.

When I called "Sam" back, he said that he was at lunch and would speak with me soon. When I heard that my manager was let go, I figured that he just wanted to make me aware of that (my eternal optimism is something I really need to work on).

So I got into the office with him and HR and they shared with me the news. Before I could even try to control it, the tears began to flow. Not just a tear or two but the type of tears that you had when you were a kid who just got a spanking and a reprimand at the same time.   So not only did your butt hurt, but your feelings were hurt as well.   There I was in the office unemployed, crying uncontrollably, and embarrassed that I was crying. Now, I have always been taught in Corporate America not to cry. In their perspective, crying is a sign of weakness; however, I have never believed that. To me, tears are a sign of strength.

Just think about all of the women who shed tears as they gave birth to their children. Think of the pain of delivery, the physical tolls on the body, and the stress of caring for this new life already on her mind. They shed the tears but kept pushing.

I think back to my mom. When my dad was battling cancer, she wouldn't let him die in the hospital. She worked third shift so my brother and I took turns caring for him while she slept or worked until his demise. She shed tears due to the hurt and frustration, but she did it anyway. She shed tears, but through them she planned his funeral, made sure he was buried with dignity, and continued providing for the family as best she could.

Through her tears, or despite her tears, she did it anyway. I believe that tears are one of the ways that the body processes emotions that are then transformed into strength to accomplish a task or a set of tasks. I will say it again: tears are a sign of strength. Even as I write this for the first time, putting my thoughts on paper, the tears are flowing, but they are being processed into strength to continue.

Think of all of the men and women alike who had to fight through chemotherapy, fight through major injuries, surviving the pain of going through the process. Each of us as individuals that have gone through the struggles to success, to live, and even to hope. When you see their tears, see the strength of them. There is no weakness in that.

LOOKING BACK!

⇐ What characteristics do you display that have a negative connotation but can be a strength?

⇐ How do you perceive those characteristics?

MOVING FORWARD!

⇒ How will you use those characteristics on your behalf?

⇒ When will you use them to benefit you?

Chapter Three

It's an Honor to Get To

As I quietly went to my desk to begin gathering my things, I looked at the many motivational and encouraging thoughts I posted in my cubical. This is where my optimism immediately kicked back in. After all, I needed to change my thoughts so I could manage my tears better. I didn't want my peers, whom I had really built strong relationships with for over three years, to see me not smiling and worse, balling uncontrollably.

"It's an honor to get to."

Every now and again, I get a chance to watch Pastor Joel Olsteen. I think he is a unique person who can deliver a message that can be very complex in a very simple manner. In one of his sermons, I heard him say, "It's an honor to get to."

That statement was so powerful to me that I wrote it on a post-it-note and affixed   it on my computer monitor at work.

While I began to take the pictures of my family and coworkers down, I began to tell God thank you because I got to. I got to meet and bond with people that would not have otherwise been in my reach. I got to learn project management and business analytics from some of the best. I got to rub elbows with vice presidents and directors.   I got to teach those that I knew were intellectually smarter than I'll ever be. I got to learn about other cultures and I got to learn more about myself. I got to. And although that time was now over, I knew that it was an honor to get to.

It could have gone a different way, where my job could have been bondage and not the freedom that it was... not expanding and growing. I have been in positions before in which the mundane repetition nearly suffocated me. But not here, not as an analyst, I got to!

Looking Back!

⇐ What were some of the positive life lessons you could learn during difficult situations?

⇐ How long did it take for you to learn those lessons?

Moving Forward!

⇒ How are you applying those life lessons?

⇒ How are you empowering others through the lessons learned?

Chapter Four

A Graceful Exit

This takes me to the next saying by Ellen Goodman that I had posted in my cube…

"There's a trick to the Graceful Exit. It begins with the vision to recognize when a job, a life stage, a relationship is over and to let go. It means leaving what's over without denying its value."

I came across this saying many years ago when I was in a job that just wasn't fulfilling to me. I would get up daily and dread going to work. I knew that there was something more for me to do, but I was struggling to get to it. I had this saying posted because I knew my time was done in that role, I recognized it clearly. It was a great opportunity for me to get into the door of this organization that had just terminated me, but it was time to move on. So I didn't want to lose or diminish the value of where I was, but I just knew it was time to move forward. I kept this saying when I moved into my new role and kept it posted the entire time because to me, it didn't apply to just work, but to life just as it said. There would be days when I would have to make decisions about situations and would look over at the saying, and ask myself, is it over? And if it is, can I leave it gracefully?

One thing about me is that I pride myself on being a lady. I certainly don't always do everything correctly but, when I walk, I walk like a lady, when I talk, I talk like a lady and when I live I live like a lady. That's truly who I am and I love me!

As I packed my desk, fighting back the tears, and thinking about the value this last position had afforded me, gratefulness began to swell inside. I began to talk to God. I am sure that if anyone was watching me or listening attentively they would have heard some mumbling and even noticed my mouth moving. I was telling Him thank you.

"Since you have allowed this to happen, God, that has to mean that you have something else, something better in store for me. I know that you wouldn't just leave me or forsake me. God, I thank you for the opportunity to serve here. I hope that someone was encouraged, uplifted and motivated by me while I was here, but since my time is up now, God, what else do you have for me?"

After an hour of packing and sorting, I realized that I didn't want to leave with everyone there and that I wouldn't be able to carry it all anyways. So I decided to take a bit that day and come back to get the remainder of my things.

While I was walking away from one thing, I wanted to begin walking into my new thing. I wanted to at least know what I was going to do next. So while I was walking to my car, I was asking the same questions … God what do you want me to do now? What's next for me? What does this mean for me?

On the drive home I began to shift my thoughts to things like: I have to tell my husband, my children; how will they react?   What sort of financial strain will this put on the household? Lord, I drive a truck and the gas prices are horrible am I going to have to get a car? Funny, I know, the things that we think of ... in all of these thoughts and emotions of this topsy-turvy day ... while my mind ran one million miles a minute, my spirit was full of peace. It was so calm that I could not believe it.

I got home and made a couple of phone calls to arrange the pick up of the remainder of my things. I went in early the next day. The team began to figure out what had happened, but I didn't want them to see me walking out with boxes. As emotional as it was for me, I couldn't imagine how it had to be for them. To have to sit and work a full day while watching those that they care about and support walk out of the building with boxes in their hands. I imagine that while they had a job, their stress level tripled. They not only have the stress of seeing people walked out, but they also have the fear of uncertainty of it being them next. Worst of all, their workloads doubled as they picked up the work of those that were let go.

So there I was, 7am the next day, collecting the remainder of my things and placing them in boxes, talking with the HR representative, "my escort," still looking to deposit. I spoke with her about what I did, and the things that I left behind. I told her that there was valuable information at the desk that could be given to someone who would find value in it.

I shared the values that I gained from life's experiences. I told her that I had been laid off or terminated (whichever term you prefer) before so I should be an old pro. She shared with me that someone else in the organization was released from their department, and was then picked up by another one in the organization and she wished that for me as well.

I packed my things and walked to the car (I didn't drive the truck; I figured I needed to begin making lifestyle changes right away). She escorted me very kindly and helped put my things in the vehicle. I got in and drove away. I immediately called my husband. I did it. It was a graceful exit. I saw the value, appreciated the value, and let it go. Driving home on the expressway, in my car and driving into my future in my mind and spirit. A graceful lady!

Looking Back!

⇐ What situations were you able to walk away from gracefully?

⇐ Were you confident that while it was time to move on, there was value in the experience?

⇐ What was the value you gained from that situation?

⇐ Were you able to walk away proud, with very little or no regret?

Moving Forward!

⇒ What will you do in the future to ensure that a graceful exit happens?

Chapter Five

Remember Your Dreams

Initially it seems unfortunate that after you have given your time your energy and your commitment to something, and in my case a company that it can be just taken from you, however, this really was a blessing for me, and I am sure any dramatic situation will also be a blessing for you. Your perspective has to be clear that there is good that can come from any situation. We just have to find what it is.

In my case, the good was that I was able to sit still for a while and go back to the foundation of who I was and what I wanted. I was able to really have the quite time to reflect on my dreams. What were they before I got busy with the hustle and bustle of life? What goals did I really want to reach before being inundated with a 50 hour work week, a family and church obligations? Did they connect with my dreams? Do I even remember by dreams for that matter?

This time enabled me to go back and look at my dreams. What were they? What are they? How does my current life align or not? What do I need to do to get accomplish them? Truthfully, before I could set the goals, I simply had to remember what they were.

My reality is that there are so many things that I would like to accomplish that I had to be realistic with myself and identify those that I was close to accomplishing and those that I was nowhere near accomplishing, that enabled me to prioritize what I should focus on first. But it all started with me remembering my dreams.

LOOKING BACK!

⇐ What are three dreams that you have?

MOVING FORWARD!

⇒ What can you do to achieve them?

Chapter Six

Sowing and Reaping

Still processing all that had happened, I was contacted by many with a very strong show of support. That is probably one of the most memorable things about that organization. They really did do a good job hiring great people. Granted, they may not have been in good job fits, but they truly were great people. I didn't realize how many thought highly of me and respected me. In life, you will reap what you sow and you have to sow to reap.

This isn't bragging, but I am confident that I have been taught well by my spiritual leader that you will reap what you sow. I know that I have sown support, love, understanding, encouragement, money, prayer, sacrifice, energy, time, and whatever else I could into those that I could. I have been taught to speak life, not only into myself, but into the lives of others. I again, am just a believer that we can succeed if and when we work together.

At work, it was often taught that you go to fulfill a job and not to make friends. While this is correct, it doesn't mean that you don't form bonds and relationships with others, because the reality is that you do. You build relationships with people, and those relationships make your job easier. Those relationships allow you to learn and grow and teach.

As they are pouring their knowledge into you, you can also pour knowledge or wisdom back into them. Many people that I worked with were engineers, sales professionals, IT professionals, even vice-presidents. They spent years in school and in the workplace learning and improving themselves to ensure that they are a commodity and provide value in whatever they do.

I had the luxury of asking them questions about how they did what they did and allowing them to pour into me. Now, I may never become any sort of engineer or salesperson, as that isn't on my to-do list, but their teaching me enabled me to better teach them. To learn their perspectives allowed me to become a better advocate for them. They were sowing into me and they were reaping the benefits by me sowing back into them.

So when the job elimination came, I had begun to reap the benefits of their support, their kind words, and even their recommendations.   I worked really closely with a colleague in a different department. Soon after he heard about this change, he immediately wrote a glowing reference for me. This was without me even asking. Sowing and Reaping.

Still Reaping

During this time, my godmother went to Denver to stay with her daughter for several weeks and had a stroke. Due to her health issues and not wanting her to worry, I didn't want to tell her that I lost my job. I didn't have the heart to tell her that her goddaughter that she was so proud of was just laid off from her job. The very one that she encouraged and supported through her master's degree program to be more marketable on her job was now without one. But in her illness, and her slurred speech she still spoke life into me. Saying that while she didn't know where God was taking me, He was, in fact, taking me higher. He was, in fact, allowing all of this to happen and it was for my own good.

Still Reaping

During this time, my spiritual leader and pastor was experiencing some challenges. I hesitated to share with him, but when I did, he also began to speak into my life. While in the middle of his trials, he began to encourage me. He told me that God has a plan for my life and that

He is going to take care of me. He let me know that everything was going to be alright. My pastor's character is so unusual to me. My pastor never said "I am sorry to hear that," or "that's too bad," he was simply in move-forward mode. He really didn't give me an opportunity to have a pity party. Maybe that's why I made such a graceful exit. Now that's a real pastor and leader.

Still Reaping

I haven't said much about my husband throughout this journey and that's because it really was my journey. While we certainly are one and we are unified, there are some experiences where you feel alone, even while others are with you.

When my husband called me on his way home from work, he asked how my day was and I tried to be as "normal" as possible. Later, he said that he could tell in my voice that something wasn't right. When he got home, I informed him of my day and his first concern was me. He wanted to know if I was ok, and of course, I said "yes,"all while the tears began to flow again. Then he asked, "What do you want to do?" I didn't really have an answer; I just really needed to process this change ... and so I didn't need to answer. I showed him all the paperwork and he hugged me. That weekend we looked at all of our expenses. We identified areas that needed to be cut and spending that would be curbed as a result of me being home, such as fast food and truck gas. He then looked at me and said, "We will be fine. If you want to go back to work, go, and if you don't, don't go. It's your choice."

Still Reaping

One of the things I do at church is expedite the offering. Expediting a church offering usually consists of whomever, saying something encouraging and uplifting with a biblical foundation to further encourage, motivate, and reinforce the importance of giving to the ministry. My husband and I are faithful tithe payers and we believe that God does reward tithers and believers. When I began to expedite, I began to talk about my job loss and how I believed God.

While I was still emotionally distressed by the situation, I was at peace and addressed it so others would also be encouraged. Regardless of your financial situation, you can still be faithful and obedient to God and remain blessed as a result. I believe that we are overcomers by the words of our testimonies. We get strength from each other. I often feel like there are too many things we try to handle on our own. One, we shouldn't, and two, we really don't have to. After service that day and since then, many have poured   out support, love, and encouragement. Whether one believes in karma, God, the universe, or whatever anyone wants to call it, I am convinced that you reap what you sow and that you have to sow to reap.

LOOKING BACK!

⇐ What have you sown to others?

⇐ Would you like to reap what you have sown?

MOVING FORWARD!

⇒ What changes will you make in order to look forward to your reaping based on your sowing ?

Chapter Seven

I Have to Take the Hard Way

So here I am, in the morning, kids are at school, husband is at work and it's just me. Going back to those questions that I asked in the beginning: What did you want me to learn? What's next for me? I began to search myself. I began to study the Word of God and I began to look at the lives of those that I admire in the world. Some of whom I may never get a chance to interact with, such as President Obama, Oprah Winfrey, TD Jakes, Joel Olsteen, just to name a few, and I began to listen to their stories.

I thought about their lives while examining my life in parallel. Asking myself what is it that I really want to do now? God, what is it that you want me to do? Are you sure you want me to do it? How will I do it? And to make matters worse, I also have to deal with the fear of the unknown. Pushing my way through the fog of anxiety, trying to listen and learn ... about me ....

When I dream, I dream big. I dream about buying both my mother and grandmother homes that they would only have to live in and not pay a dime. I dream of paying for my kids' college education with ease to further empower them to be the very best. I dream of opening a Youth Education Facility that would provide educational resources as well as entertainment that would help get and keep adolescences out of trouble and provide jobs for the community.

I dream of helping my ministry grow stronger, and building the Fine Arts Theater that my pastor has dreamed of for years. I have a nice sized home now, but I dream of ten-thousand square feet with a Segway for room to room mobility. I dream of heated floors, a walk-in closet with a rotating closet system, and staff to help maintain it. Yes, I dream big.

I learned that while it would be easy to go back to Corporate America, in order for my dreams to come true, I have to take the hard way. I have to take chances and do things that I have never done. I have to take risks to reap the rewards of them.

When I look at Oprah Winfrey, she wasn't always where she is today; she started somewhere. Well, this is my somewhere start. I have learned that going the hard way is just that hard! But when I reflect on my life there were many times that I chose the difficult route ... and they proved to provide the most reward, such as getting married at eighteen and staying married.

I came from a very loving two-parent home and during difficult times, I could have just walked away from my marriage and pretended that it never happened, but that would have been the easy way.

Another example, going for my MBA. I could have just stayed satisfied with my bachelor's and not even considered moving forward, but that would have been the easy way. I could have said, "I am going to wait until the kids get older" or "I am going to wait until my job load gets lighter" or I could have simply said "I don't want to." That would have been the easy way. Instead, I chose the sleepless nights, the long days of work and school, and the days of work, kids, homework, and husband. There were so many invitations I had to decline because I had a paper due or had to study. That was definitely the hard way.

The point is, to maintain my lifestyle, I would simply take the easy way in doing what I already know I am good at and not taking any risks. However, if I want my dreams to come true, I have to do some things that I have never done. I have to sacrifice time watching television, or time doing menial tasks, or money. This is where I encourage you to do the same.

LOOKING BACK!

⇐ What activities have you discontinued so that you can reallocate that time to achieving your goals?

MOVING FORWARD!

⇒ What activities are you doing to achieve your goals?

I challenge you to make a plan to move toward your dreams using your reality to get there. Yes, it is certainly the hard way, but you can do it. We can do it!

Chapter Eight

Plan B

As you are planning your dreams and how to accomplish them through your reality, begin to also ensure that you have a Plan B. We should always have a safety net or something to fall back on. Sometimes people are so focused on one thing that they don't consider anything else. I am sure there are tons of athletes that were awesome at their craft, but were injured. Now what do they do? What was their Plan B?

Right now my Plan B is my husband (thanks honey). He and I understand that we are one unit and as I pursue my dreams, his support and love has been amazing. With that said, there may come a time during this pursuit that I may need to return to work, but if I do, it will not keep me from my dream, it will just make the hard way a bit harder. But hey, if I can work a full-time job, raise two kids, keep my husband happy, cook, clean, attend school full-time, and be a fairly active participant at church, I am sure I can do this.

LOOKING BACK!

⟸ What's your Plan A?

⟸ What is your Plan B?

MOVING FORWARD!

⟹ What tools and resources are you using to execute your plans?

Asking these questions will help prepare you for your graceful exit if that's necessary. Think about your plans, invest in them wisely, and watch the returns.

Chapter Nine

Investments

Now, while making my dreams come true I also have to live in reality. This means that I can't spend like a big baller (as the young people say). I have to be wise and frugal. I have to invest wisely so that I don't take a loss. The term "investing" is usually used when speaking about financial matters, but investing is really more about how you are using anythingthat you perceive as valuable. Let's use time as an example.

Time

Time is one commodity used daily that we will never be able to get back. How we invest our time is critical to our dream and our reality. I am excited about the possibility of being a published author, instead of spending my time watching television, I am spending it learning how to write, market, and publish a book. Instead of spending my time surfing the internet, I have learned that there are very reputable colleges that offer access to free courses, so I am taking advantage of an education that would enhance me.

Children

There is something else worthy of investment: our children. After a hard day's work and/or school, the last thing we may want to do is deal with little ones. Even if your dreams don't come true, as a parent you have the responsibility and I would even say obligation to provide at the minimum the structure and framework for your children to grow and succeed.

That's done by making sure their homework is done, making sure they know and understand right and wrong, being sure that they know it is their job to be better than you ... yes, I said it. Better. However great you are, your kids should be better, smarter, and a positive contribution to society. I think we are way past our quota for menaces. As parents, we have the power and authority to change the world by changing our children one child at a time. So when you think of an investment that has the propensity to return a million times over, our children is that investment.

In retrospect, I see that I have a plan b, c, and d ... Plan B—My husband, Plan C—Going back to my prior type of work, and Plan D—My children. I am such an over preparer. One of the largest reasons that many do not realize their dreams is due to the lack of finances. However, I want to prompt us to look at that challenge in a different light.

I often hear people say that they can't go back to school because they don't have the money. They will take a loan out with a monthly payment for a car, they will run up all types of credit cards for clothing, shoes, and televisions, but they will not invest in their education. They will not invest in the area in which they have passion and vision. I believe that methodology is backward.

I have a relative that I have been encouraging to pursue her basic education for some time. During our last interaction, she spoke of the same financial challenge. In an attempt to motivate her and remove any excuses, I offered to pay for her to go back to school. Her role was to get the cost information to me and go. She verbally committed to me that she would call me with the information, but she never did. She did call me several weeks later to ask if I was still willing to fund her education. Although irritated by the delay, I still said yes. The time between our first and second interaction, I went from a full-time employee to unemployed. Needless to say I haven't heard from her again. I reiterate, others usually are willing to invest in you, but you have to be willing to invest in yourself.

In hindsight, I am glad that she didn't pursue further if she wasn't committed. When you get committed to your passion, to your dream, you will be amazed at all the free business seminars, opportunities, and overall support that you will encounter. Go to the discount bookstore, get used books. Go to the library, borrow them. There are many ways to get to accomplish your desired goals.

Also there are so many web sites in which you can propose your dream and have others sow into it with you. These are great opportunities to utilize your resources and allow them to have a vested interest in your success.

I spoke earlier about living modestly. Some may find that difficult to believe considering I have a luxury SUV and a nice sized home. Modesty in my mind is the awareness of how and where I'm spending my money. For example, on Sundays, I invest $1.00 in a newspaper and cut coupons. When I want fast food, I look to eat where I have a coupon for. If I get two dollars off my meal, then I have paid for my newspaper and saved 1.00. This is just with one coupon. Imagine if I had five, six, or ten. Yes, it takes time to organize but if you save what you would normally spend, then those monies can be reallocated into your dream. I also tap into the online resources such as Daily Deals, Living Social and many others.

When we had two incomes coming into the household, it wasn't a big deal to pay full price because we had it. But the truth is, I should have been a better steward when I had more. This experience is also teaching me to be a better manager.

Consider another perspective from a biblical perspective. Think back to the story of when Jesus took two fish, and five loaves of bread and fed the multitude. Multitude being five-thousand men and then add on the women and children. Jesus was able to take what was less than enough and make more than enough. So much so, that there were even leftovers.

With the knowledge that with God anything is possible and with the resources that have been placed on this earth for us, I ask myself, "What's holding us back?"

I wonder if our lack of success is due not to finances or any other external factor, but the internal factors. What's in the heart of us that we can't or won't drive toward success? Who have we allowed to define success for us? I hate to admit it, but when I lost my job, I was embarrassed. My husband and I, the power couple in Corporate America had just lost half our power. Both of us working at fortune 100 companies, making good money and in less than five minutes, it all changed. But who said that I lost my power? Who determines my worth? Why is it that I felt that I lost part of me when I lost my job? Who gave my job that much authority in my life? I did, that's who.

Things that defined me were my faith, my family, and my job. However, when the tides changed I needed to redefine myself. And I did. It was difficult, but I still did it. I needed to realize that my job was what I did, not who I was. Now, in my defense, there were several aspects of my job that reflected me perfectly, but those aspects or characteristics are very transferable, so even in that, I needed to create a line of delineation.

LOOKING BACK!

⇐ What is it about you that you feel you can't achieve difficult goals?

⇐ Is there anything really holding us back besides ourselves?

⇐ What's holding you back?

MOVING FORWARD!

⇒ What are you going to do about your obstacle?

⇒ How are you going to overcome your obstacle?

Chapter Ten

Maybe Another-Time

It's funny that I never thought that I would leave that company. It was my plan to be there most of my career or until my realities caught my dreams.   The truth is I don't think that my realities would have ever caught me there.   I was so confident that that was where I was supposed to be that some of the passwords to my accounts were "the company name" 4life.

There were nights that I literally did not sleep so that I could meet deadlines. There were times I would work all day, come home and feed and take care of the family and then work for two, three, four more hours so I could stay ahead. This type of dedication can only be focused in one area. That's why I don't believe that my dreams would have ever caught my realities. My focus wasn't on

One of the things that I taught my kids was "not now doesn't mean not ever." This then was translated into "maybe another time." When my kids were toddlers and we went to the store, they would see something they wanted. Sometimes I would say yes and sometimes I would say no. Of course at their age they didn't care for the word "no" so the tantrums would ensue. I would immediately redirect them by having them repeat after me... "Maybe another time." That way they understood that just because they couldn't have it on that day, that didn't mean that they couldn't ever have it.

I was in the representative role that I was positive I had outgrown and was miserable in. I remember trying to leave the organization. Interview after interview outside the company, but nothing seemed to pan out. I remember knowing that although I was looking to leave, it wasn't the time to do so. I just felt a "no" regarding that. Ironically, I remember when I was initially called to interview for the analyst role, I had to decline the initial date and time due to an outside interview. When I did finally interview and was called back for a second interview I was ecstatic. I just knew that it was God. It took about a month to get the position offered to me. I was standing on eggshells not knowing what was happening. When it finally came through, the new role resulted in a significant salary increase, along with the new challenges and opportunities I had desired.

Soon after, I moved into my last role there as an analyst. And oh, how I loved my job. From that experience I heard the "no" in regard to the company change, but I forgot the "maybe another time." That is, until the time came. I had to release that company in which I was so attached. And I say that as if I had a choice. So let me clarify; they didn't ask me if I wanted to be terminated - they terminated me. I often wonder if that was my biggest challenge – they took my option to leave.

So I have learned not to get too attached. I am not sure how many people will begin working for a company today and still be with them in 30 years. While I am hoping they are out there, I am just not sure that if the company is around in 30 years, they will have kept you, me, or Joe the plumber on board.

LOOKING BACK!

⇐ What are you attached to that you may need to loosen?

⇐ What are you holding on to, although this may be the time to let go?

MOVING FORWARD!

⇒ What steps will you take to move forward?

Chapter Eleven

Seeking Wise Counsel

About nine months before the layoff occurred, I went to my manager, excited about all the great performance reviews I had received, hitting the three-year mark in the same position, I thought that this would be a great time to ask for a promotion. I wanted a promotion in title to recognize that I had grown in my role and had been successful. For three years I had been an analyst I, and had done quite well so I thought. This was in June. July, August, and September passed and there was no response. So I followed up. Several more weeks had passed and, again, no response.

In my mind, what's so difficult about changing an analyst I to an analyst II? During all of this, other transitions began to take place. Outside consultants came in and began to analyze the business. Reviewing how we do what we do and looking for areas of efficiency. Prioritizing any suggested changes. Although the results indicated some major restructuring, I never thought my role would be impacted because I was part of the technology team. Simultaneously, I was approached about another position. One that I thought was quite intriguing and would stretch me even further. I discussed it with my manager and then decided to post for it. I didn't get the job but my manager's comments soon after were "We were going to give you a raise but since you posted for another position we are not going to."

Needless to say, I was fuming and for a few reasons: 1) I never asked for a raise, I simply wanted acknowledgement. 2) You're telling me "no" in November and your reasoning is due to an opportunity to better myself. I was so hurt and bothered. I just couldn't believe it.

One morning, during this period, I was sitting at my desk and "Sandra" came across something that she perceived as disturbing. She came to get me. "Sandra" took me to the mailroom and began to explain that she was looking for an envelope to send out some mail and on the top shelf in the cabinet she came across something with my name on it. It was my five year service award with the company.

Celebrating five years – something that the company perceived as a milestone, but my award was in a cabinet with the envelopes. Now I thought about this a couple of different ways:

1)   My manager is virtual; he could have been waiting to present it at some event. –But if so, why wouldn't he have given it to someone for safe keeping?

2)   My manager knows and has admitted that his management skills aren't the best, so why wouldn't he have just walked it to my desk and said congrats, or left it for me to see the next day? Something other than somebody just coincidentally finding something that I earned. While these challenges could have been worse; they were still emotionally stressful for me.

In my frustration, I began writing documented response to these occurrences that I was planning to send to both he and his manager. After my husband read it, he told me not to send it. So I didn't. While I can't remember exactly what I said, I do remember the tone in which I said it in. I had to then go and seek counsel from a very trusted adviser of mine. I could go and sit at his home and share with him and his wife what I was experiencing and receive guidance.

My counsel shared with me that I had to be still, and do not allow people to get me that angry that I cost myself a job. He shared with me that I have to remember that I serve God and that everything will be alright. I had to listen to wisdom, wise counsel.

Wisdom doesn't come from a perfect life, it comes from experience. Take advantage of anything that can be shared to make your life easier and maintains your integrity if applied.

Soon after, I was approached about two other possible opportunities but I didn't even apply for them simply because that experience had me fearful of the backlash.

Isn't fear a funny thing? I allowed fear to cause me to fail because I didn't even try. Please do not allow fear to keep you from trying.

I am not sure what triggered this next conversation, but something did and I spoke with my manager's former manager. Let's call him "Joe." I shared with "Joe" these happenings and his wisdom was to change job roles within the company. I just passed up two opportunities and one of the people that I deeply respect and admire tells me to move.

Maybe, had I sought wise counsel sooner, instead of relying on my optimism and work ethic, my stress would not have been so high. But at least it was a lesson learned; take advantage of wise counsel.

LOOKING BACK!

⇐ Who is your wise counsel for difficult situations in life?

⇐ Who is your counsel for your career advancement?

⇐ How do you know that the counsel that you are receiving is wise?

MOVING FORWARD!

⇒ What sort of improvements have you seen after you applied the counsel to your life?

Chapter Twelve

Strengths and Weaknesses

In reading about some of my experiences with my manager, your first impression may be that he was not the greatest. The truth is, that while he had some weaknesses, he certainly had many strengths. There were many instances in which he was very flexible with my scheduling; he was very giving of his time and support. In addition, he was brilliant in his craft. I guess we can't be perfect.

When it came to the projects, and his IT, IS experience, I believe he was exceptional. Smart like you wouldn't believe. However, his management of people needed the attention that his other skillsets had.

In a prior position with a former company I was a bank teller. I was great at it... I built strong relationships with my customers, I could make sales goals, and I could help drive success throughout the company. As a result, I was promoted to supervisor. I believe this is a problem that we run into throughout companies everywhere. The assumption is made that because you can do the job well, you can manage people well. It isn't really treated as though it's a different job and believe me when I say that it is. Individuals may have very natural leadership abilities; they need to be honed and crafted, and molded. Like any sports star, their gifts have to be developed.

Many managers/supervisors (like myself) that I have worked for were promoted, but without the training on how to manage people. I would even suggest that this training take place prior to the promotion and then followed up after the move into the new role. This training should include difficult conversations, just as it would include how to complete a performance review.

Whether this is implemented from a corporate perspective, individuals should tap into the areas on their own to be great in their craft. No one is perfect by all means, but surely if you recognize the areas in which improvements are made and set goals to accomplish them, those weaker areas will not be so glaring.

Looking Back!

⇐ Identify two weaknesses and two strengths you've observed in a person significant to you.

⇐ Identify two weaknesses and two strengths in yourself?

Moving Forward!

⇒ What can you do to compliment them in their growth/development to mitigate their weaknesses?

⇒ What can you do to compliment them in their growth/development to mitigate your weaknesses?

Chapter Thirteen

Work Your Plan

When I moved into my analyst role, I said that I would commit to it for one year and then go on to complete my master's degree. Although the role was challenging and the family was growing, it was important that I honor my commitment. Besides that, I received the benefit of receiving tuition reimbursement for each of the courses. So I did.

After about a year in the role, I enrolled into school, and just added another hat to my arsenal of things to accomplish. There I was, working full time, fairly active in ministry, a wife, mother, friend, babysitter, and so on

... but I was determined. It was critical to me to pursue and achieve my degree, because I understood that if I was going to be truly marketable, I needed that certificate.

This challenge of going to school and being committed to education, while being committed to so many other areas felt impossible sometimes, but I did it. I say "I" very loosely. It was done through the support of my husband, family; even my job. Even more, the financial support of my job was vital. I took full advantage of their tuition reimbursement opportunities. If I received a B or higher, my courses were paid for. And they were. Even after I had been terminated, there were two more classes that they reimbursed me for.

Thinking back, what if I hadn't begun and completed school as scheduled? Then I would have been financially responsible for the courses, the learning, and I would be at a disadvantage without a degree today. Sometimes I wonder if that was one of the core purposes of my position, to promote me academically. Once that was accomplished, my purpose within the organization was accomplished.

LOOKING BACK!

⇐ What plans have you made that you have yet to commit to achieving?

MOVING FORWARD!

⇒ What plans will you commit to?

What opportunities will you take advantage of once you realize that they are being offered?

Chapter Fourteen

Embracing You

In an earlier chapter, I made mention that I like who I am. I think knowing, embracing, and liking who you are, is critical in every facet of life. Physically, I am full of flaws and imperfections, emotionally, I am probably perceived the same by others, and intellectually, there are some areas I am pretty good in and many that I am horrible in. But that's who I am. To make matters better or worse, depending on your perspective, those characteristics are yet evolving daily. I also believe that those are the very things setting me apart from anyone else.

Those are the things that I focus on. For example, I often get compliments on my speaking abilities, so whenever I get an opportunity, I try to be as prepared as possible to present a compelling argument in whatever topic I am focusing on. When I am having an "emotional day," I usually will communicate that ... "Hey guys I am having a rough day...." Things that I am not good at, I tap into people, and not only learn, but more importantly, allow them to operate in their area of expertise. That's who I am. I understand that I don't have to know everything and do everything. I understand that two are better than one, and I take full advantage of that.

At my church I have been given the opportunity and privilege to write and direct plays. I have a team of great innovators, and creative minds that work with me. Not only that, but what I love most about this auxiliary is the ability to bring people from completely different backgrounds and upbringings together.

The fine arts department strengthens the unity while learning and embracing the diversity of our backgrounds. Also this is where you will find those that may never sing a solo part with the choir. Those that may never speak over the pulpit get into character. It's just amazing to watch. I can use the fine arts department to facilitate that. This is who I am. This is what I love and I work to make me better at it.

Understanding, embracing, and liking who you are while very aware that you can still be better, can further help you make your dreams a reality.

Tap into you; don't be afraid. I believe that if you don't like you, you have the power to change you! The changes that you make should also be for you and not others. Usually the reason we don't like ourselves is because we don't know who we are. We have spent so much time trying to be what and who someone else wants us to be that we don't really know ourselves.

To be completely transparent, being who you are can be very scary as well. None of us like rejection, none of us like to be criticized and, deep down, we just want to be loved and appreciated. The fear of being rejected or unloved due to being our true self can become overwhelming. I want to give you a different perspective. If you are not operating as your "true you," you don't have to worry about rejection from anyone else because you have already rejected yourself. Not only that, but you are preventing someone else from being exposed to the great things that the real you has to offer.

LOOKING BACK!

⇐ Who are you?

⇐ What do you bring to the table?

⇐ What sets you apart?

⇐ What do you love to do?

MOVING FORWARD!

⇒ What qualities would you like to improve upon?

⇒ What qualities will you embrace?

⇒ What other things would you like to try to do?

⇒ What are your next three major goals in twelve months, and three years?

Chapter Fifteen

Starting From Scratch

Throughout any transition any of must make, it is imperative that even when we feel as though we are starting from scratch, we recognize that we are not. Every experience, every set back, every thrust forward, there are some lessons in each of them that can be used to better prepare you for the next opportunity ahead of you. While I was maximizing this downtime, I was able to strengthen relationships, I was able to focus on specific skills and build on them, and I was able to learn more about myself. So while starting from scratch seems as though it's a negative thing, you really aren't starting from scratch so celebrate that.

I am sure there are some that will argue that you are starting from scratch with a new job, just as I did when I started a new job. However although the job was new, the experiences that I brought with me, even if it was in a different industry helped. For example, when I worked in banking, I had to do quite a bit of reconciliations for cash variances. In those instances, my ability to focus on deposit slips, withdrawal slips as well as my ability to read and study spreadsheets of data was critical. When I moved into the IT space, those skills helped me tremendously as I performed data analytics. So remember, your not starting from scratch. Never underestimate all that you bring to the table and don't be afraid to use it to bring about improvements.

Chapter Sixteen

Fear

Throughout this book, I have spoken about fear. I was afraid to do this, and afraid to do that. It just, (yes at this moment) dawned on me ... I have to treat fear like tears. I have to accept it, embrace it and then do what I need to do. If tears don't stop women from giving birth, if tears didn't stop my mom from burying my dad, then fear shouldn't stop me from moving forward in my life.

Fear is now my motivation. My motivation to be the very best, fear is now saying that this situation could work out really badly or it is also saying this could be really good. Before the execution of my decision, fear is prompting me to think whether the risk is worth the reward. I think that's what it's designed to do. Not to stop you but to make sure you consider the consequences.

If I am going to fear failure, then I should also fear success. I see so many public figures that, in my mind, are successful due to their prestige, finance, and their popularity, who are also getting divorces, going to jail, and/or are now getting negative press. So what will success do to me or for me? Will it help my children, marriage, family, church, and community just as I desire it to? Or will it hurt them?

I don't really have the answer to that but I do know that my faith keeps me grounded, my family keeps me humble, and my past keeps me flexible. It was similar to work. I was in a cubical with a "secure" job on Tuesday and filing for unemployment on Wednesday.

LOOKING BACK!

⇐ How do you define fear?

⇐ What are you fearful of?

⇐ What do you think would happen if you faced your fear?

MOVING FORWARD!

⇒ How will you overcome your fear?

⇒ How will you make it work for you?

Chapter Seventeen

Show Appreciation

Spouse

At four-years-old, I met a little boy at school that would chase me and push me down on the playground. He would steal his mother's jewelry and give it to me. At eighteen, I married that same little boy who has been nothing but good to me. We have grown up together and bonded, and we are raising our children together. We love each other so passionately that we don't even sleep well when we are apart.

I think back to him right around my first lay off/termination. We had just built our first home from the ground up. Four bedrooms, 2.5 bathrooms, living room, dining room, kitchen, office-the middle-class dream is what I'll call it. We did it at thirty-years-old. We moved in to our home on his thirty-first birthday. In June of that year, I was notified that my job was being eliminated and that I would need to post for other positions in the organization or accept the severance package.

In speaking with my husband he said, "Stay home, finish school; I believe it is going to be you that will take us to the next level financially." I did just that. I stayed home and went to school until I had to go back to work. I had two classes to finish when I went back to work and finished them successfully to receive my bachelors of arts in business management and communication. After I completed school, he then went on and completed school a year later with the same degree.

Growing up as a child, I had a mother and a father who put the kids first. At that age, I was blessed enough to have a husband that did the same thing. Most of this book has spoken about life lessons that I have learned and have been reinforced throughout my career, but I wanted to also make mention that there is a man that God has given me that has allowed me, supported me, and put this household in a place financially, that I can continue to chase my dreams. This certainly doesn't take away from the support of my family, friends, and many others that I haven't mentioned or alluded to but this is to acknowledge him: my Spouse

Mom

I have never really been too sure how my mom felt about me. Her words very seldom, and I mean very seldom, indicated (at least to me) whether she was proud of my accomplishments. But her actions did. I remember going on field trips in elementary school with the biggest lunch because my mom would fix my lunch so that if anyone else forgot their lunch, I could share with them. I remember her coming up to the school and playing double- dutch rope with me and my friends.

I even remember a time when I was molested by my grandfather's brother and I came home and told my mother. The very next day in church, she threatened him. This is how it went: We were sitting together in church and she said to me ... "Is that him?"; I said "yes."

Immediately after dismissal she went up to him with me right next to her and said ... "You touched my daughter!" He proceeded to say that he didn't know what he had done because he had been drinking and not himself since the death of his sister. My mom then said ... "Touch my baby again and you will be right up there with her!"

I thought my mother walked on water. As I rewind the time in my mind, I can clearly see all the times that demonstrated that she loved me and was proud of me. She attended every graduation, even the college ones. If I was a key speaker at events, she would attend. If I needed a babysitter, she was there. She even kept my son for about the first year of his life. He is spoiled to death to this day. Thanks ma!

She was there when my spouse and I married at the courthouse. She was there when my spouse and I celebrated our ten year wedding anniversary and renewed our wedding vows at a church. She has been there.   She exemplifies the mother and woman that I strive to be everyday.

I don't think, as children, we can even fathom the sacrifice that parents make until we are parents ourselves.   In keeping with my earlier position, your kids, or our kids should be better.   My mom has made me better and supported me throughout the process.

Grandmother

We are often so critical of those that are close to us. As kids, we say, "when I grow up I am going to do things differently." "I am going to do things the right way," but the reality is that they did the best they could with what they had and with what they knew.

Recently, I was talking to my grandmother about my son and some of the challenges that I was having. I then said that he needed a spanking. She jumped in and said, "No, don't spank him; we have now learned a better way."

I thought that was such a profound statement from an over seventy-year-old woman, who was the "evil mother" that would wake my aunts and uncles up with spankings for not following directions. In that statement, she also taught me that you are never too old to learn, change, and adapt. She did things one way, but she is open and willing to teach and do them in a different way today.

My grandmother and mother have always been hard workers. My grandmother worked second shift to ensure that the ends were met. Their work ethic is so strong that it's still unbelievable to me sometimes. I remember mornings where one of my kids were sick and I would be calling for medical advice with the plans of not going to work that day. My grandmother would quickly say, "don't miss work; I am on my way."

I sort of laugh now at that statement because here I am unemployed after years of putting my time in. There I was, going into the office early, staying late, working nights and weekends, and being loyal to my job but my job was not loyal to me.

Show Appreciation

As you close the gap between your dreams and reality, acknowledge those that have helped you get there. Not just when you are there, but even as you are on your way. Don't forget to say "thank you." Don't forget to show appreciation. Don't forget that they were there during the ups and the downs. Not to say that you owe everyone a new car, but it is to say you can at least give gratitude.

Looking Back!

⇐ Who were or are the cheerleaders in your life? Who do you need to say "thank you" to?

Moving Forward!

⇒ What can you do to show your appreciation for their support?

⇒ When will you show your appreciation?

Here I Am!

Here I am, at the conclusion of this book; glad that I could move past my apprehension and get it finished. Glad that here I see my dream become a reality. Here I am praying that someone is blessed and encouraged by it. Here I am looking forward to the next one already. Here I am saying thank you: Thank you!

QUICK ORDER FORM

Looking Back, then Moving Forward!

List price $11.95

website: www.celestecuffie.com

For speaking engagements, or seminars, interviews, email, requests to the address listed above.

This page is intentionally left blank.

This page is intentionally left blank.

This page is intentionally left blank.

This page is intentionally left blank.

This page is intentionally left blank.

This page is intentionally left blank.

Made in the
USA
Columbia, SC